BASKETBALL LEGENDS

Kareem Abdul-Jabbar
Charles Barkley
Larry Bird
Kobe Bryant
Wilt Chamberlain
Clyde Drexler
Julius Erving
Patrick Ewing
Kevin Garnett
Anfernee Hardaway
Tim Hardaway
The Head Coaches
Grant Hill
Juwan Howard
Allen Iverson
Magic Johnson
Michael Jordan
Shawn Kemp
Jason Kidd
Reggie Miller
Alonzo Mourning
Hakeem Olajuwon
Shaquille O'Neal
Gary Payton
Scottie Pippen
David Robinson
Dennis Rodman
John Stockton
Keith Van Horn
Antoine Walker
Chris Webber

CHELSEA HOUSE PUBLISHERS

KAREEM ABDUL-JABBAR

Helen Borrello

Introduction by
Chuck Daly

CHELSEA HOUSE PUBLISHERS

Philadelphia

Produced by Daniel Bial Agency
New York, New York.

Picture research by Alan Gottlieb
Cover illustration by Alan Reingold

3 5 7 9 8 6 4

Borrello, Helen A.
    Kareem Abdul Jabbar / Helen A. Borrello.
      p.   cm. — (Basketball legends)
    Includes bibliographical references and index.
    ISBN 0-7910-2426-1 (hard)
    1. Abdul-Jabbar, Kareem, 1947– —Juvenile literature.
    2. Basketball players—United States—Biography—Juvenile literature.
    [1. Abdul-Jabbar, Kareem, 1947–. 2. Basketball players.
    3. Afro-Americans—Biography.]   I. Title. II. Series.
    GV884.A24B67 1994
    796.323'092—dc20
    [B]   94-5774
                                                              CIP
                                                               AC

CONTENTS

BECOMING A
BASKETBALL LEGEND

Chuck Daly

What does it take to be a basketball superstar? Two of the three things it takes are easy to spot. Any great athlete must have excellent skills and tremendous dedication. The third quality needed is much harder to define, or even put in words. Others call it leadership or desire to win, but I'm not sure that explains it fully. This third quality relates to the athlete's thinking process, a certain mentality and work ethic. One can coach athletic skills, and while few superstars need outside influence to help keep them dedicated, it is possible for a coach to offer some well-timed words in order to keep that athlete fully motivated. But a coach can do no more than appeal to a player's will to win; how much that player is then capable of ensuring victory is up to his own internal workings.

In recent times, we have been fortunate to have seen some of the best to play the game. Larry Bird, Magic Johnson, and Michael Jordan had all three components of superstardom in full measure. They brought their teams to numerous championships, and made the players around them better. (They also made their coaches look smart.)

I myself coached a player who belongs in that class, Isiah Thomas, who helped lead the Detroit Pistons to consecutive NBA crowns. Isiah is not tall—he's just over six feet—but he could do whatever he wanted with the ball. And what he wanted to do most was lead and win.

All the players I mentioned above and those whom this

series will chronicle are tremendously gifted athletes, but for the most part, you can't play professional basketball at all unless you have excellent skills. And few players get to stay on their team unless they are willing to dedicate themselves to improving their talents even more, learning about their opponents, and finding a way to join with their teammates and win.

It's that third element that separates the good player from the superstar, the memorable players from the legends of the game. Superstars know when to take over the game. If the situation calls for a defensive stop, the superstars stand up and do it. If the situation calls for a key pass, they make it. And if the situation calls for a big shot, they want the ball. They don't want the ball simply because of their own glory or ego. Instead they know—and their teammates know—that they are the ones who can deliver, regardless of the pressure.

The words "legend" and "superstar" are often tossed around without real meaning. Taking a hard look at some of those who truly can be classified as "legends" can provide insight into the things that brought them to that level. All of them developed their legacy over numerous seasons of play, even if certain games will always stand out in the memories of those who saw them. Those games typically featured amazing feats of all-around play. No matter how great the fans thought the superstars, the players were capable yet of surprising them, their opponents, and occasionally even themselves. The desire to win took over, and with their dedication and athletic skills already in place, they were capable of the most astonishing achievements.

CHUCK DALY, most recently the head coach of the New Jersey Nets, guided the Detroit Pistons to two straight NBA championships, in 1989 and 1990. He earned a gold medal as coach of the 1992 U.S. Olympic basketball team—the so-called "Dream Team"—and was inducted into the Pro Basketball Hall of Fame in 1994.

1
NOTHING STOPS KAREEM

Oh, no! It couldn't be happening again! Couldn't the Lakers ever beat the Celtics? For the past six times the two teams had met in the National Basketball Association finals, the Boston team had always won. The last defeat was a devastating 111-102 loss to the Celtics in the seventh game of the 1984 championships. All during the 1984-85 season, the Los Angeles team looked forward to a rematch. But the first game of the 1985 finals turned into a rout: The Celtics won by a score of 148-114. The Lakers seemed to be giving away yet another world championship title to Boston.

Something had to be done. And the man who took charge was a 38-year old center who had played 14 years of professional basketball. You might think that the stress and strain over

---

In 1985, at age 38, Kareem Abdul-Jabbar was able to lead his Los Angeles Lakers to another championship title. Here he scores despite being double-teamed by the Celtics' Robert Parish (left) and Kevin McHale.

the years would have tired the man. Or that he would have been satisfied by all the titles he had won and records he had set. He had been named the NBA's most valuable player six times, had been a member of three NBA world-championship teams, and was the all-time leading scorer in the NBA. Wouldn't he be content to let one of his younger teammates such as James Worthy, Byron Scott, Michael Cooper, or especially the dynamic Magic Johnson, take the reigns of leadership? No, Kareem Abdul-Jabbar was determined to win, and took it upon himself to unite and motivate his team.

In a team meeting, Kareem assumed blame for the Laker loss and promised to improve his own poor Game One performance. At 7'2", Kareem was a towering physical presence both on and off the court. But perhaps even more compelling was his focused expression and calm demeanor. After Game One, Kareem's manner conveyed an intense resolve. His careful words and determined spirit helped revive and inspire his teammates.

A tougher and more aggressive Laker team hit the Boston parquet to play the second game. The Lakers began successfully to execute the fast break offense for which they were renowned. Kareem's determination translated into 30 points and 17 rebounds. With a strong second-half performance by their leader, Larry Bird, the Celtics managed to reduce the Laker lead to four points with just over four minutes remaining in the game. But, in a critical moment, Kareem blocked a shot by forward Kevin McHale and sunk one of his trademark skyhooks. The shot not only extended Los Angeles's lead, it also placed Kareem's name in the record books for most points scored in the playoffs. His 4,458 points moved him ahead of Jerry West. The Lakers achieved a 109-102 win over Boston.

Kareem's strong all-around Game Two performance defied critics who had complained that he was too old for pro basketball. After the game, Kareem commented on his own performance and referred to his critics in his typically understated manner. "It feels good to know that you're not dead," he said. "They had people throwing dirt on my face. And it's good to know that was a little premature."

Having rallied to win what Laker coach Pat Riley described as the "one monumental backs-against-the-wall breakthrough game" in the years that his team had been together, the Lakers were back in the series.

Kareem performed brilliantly again in the third game, this time scoring 26 points, grabbing 14 rebounds and adding 7 assists in the Laker's win.

Although the Lakers lost Game Four by two points, they did not lose their spirit; they came back to win Game Five by a score of 120-111. The victory was aided by Kareem's spectacular defense. In the first quarter, Kareem contained center Robert Parish. In the second quarter, Riley asked Kareem to guard McHale, who had already scored 16 points. After the switch, McHale managed only three shots for the rest of the game.

The Lakers presented President Ronald Reagan with a team cap and autographed ball when he invited them to the White House following their 1985 victory. Kareem stood behind the President, between Mitch Kupchak and Coach Pat Riley.

The teams were back in Boston for Game Six. The Celtics had never lost a world championship title in the Garden; the avid Boston fans thought they were invincible at home. But the Lakers were eager to change the course of basketball history. Although Kareem and Magic spent a lot of time on the bench after getting into foul trouble, the Lakers were able to keep up with the Celtics. The first half of the sixth game ended in a 55-55 tie. In the second half, Kareem scored 18 points. Although he fouled out with 14 seconds remaining in the game, Kareem left the court knowing that the 1985 title belonged to him and his fellow Lakers.

Following the 111-100 win, an unusually buoyant Kareem poured champagne over teammates. "This is my third series against Boston and we lost in the seventh game both times," he said afterwards. "So it is real nice to come back and get into this one. Celtic pride was in the building, but so were we." Kareem returned with the rest of the Lakers to Los Angeles to a parade in which thousands of people from many different neighborhoods and walks of life came together to honor and cheer their team. June 11, 1985, the date of the parade, was officially proclaimed "Laker Day" by Los Angeles Mayor Tom Bradley.

Kareem was the unanimous choice for most valuable player in the championship series. Talking about Kareem's performance in the playoffs, Magic Johnson said, "He amazes me. But then again, he doesn't, because he's Kareem. He was focusing in. Nobody and nothing stops Kareem once his back hits the wall." Kareem's continued leadership and all-around playing ability would help the Lakers win consecutive NBA championship titles in 1987 and 1988. But it is this hard-fought-for victory over Boston that Kareem remembers as the highlight of his extraordinary pro career.

2

GROWING UP, STANDING OUT

Ferdinand Lewis Alcindor, Jr., was born on April 16, 1947 in New York City. When he was three years old, Lew—as Kareem was then called—and his parents moved from Harlem to Inwood, an area located on the northern tip of Manhattan. Lew and his parents dwelled in a middle-class housing development until after Lew's graduation from high school.

His parents' deeply-rooted self respect and dignity influenced Lew from an early age. Although an only child, Lew met many playmates in the family-oriented apartment complex; some of them are still his close friends. And since families of many different backgrounds lived in the complex, Lew learned to appreciate and respect cultural differences among people. Wooded parks near to the complex gave Lew a vast outdoor world to explore. And, as Lew got older, the train that ran next to

In elementary school, Lew Alcindor was gawky and uncoordinated. He was more interested in swimming and baseball than in basketball.

his apartment afforded him access to the many other parts of New York City in which school, sports, and social activities took place.

Music and baseball were two of Lew's earliest loves. Sounds of jazz and classical music always filled his home. His parents had met in North Carolina, where they sang in the same choir. Lew's father studied conducting, piano, and trombone at the Juilliard School of Music; when he was five, Lew attended his father's graduation from the college. His father worked as a corrections officer and then as a Transit Authority policeman, since opportunities for black symphony conductors and players were rare. Despite his father's reserve, Lew recognized his passion for music, a passion that Lew began to share. From an early age, Lew attended jazz jam sessions in which his father played. As he got older, Lew spent hours listening to jazz in his room, and he and his friends would frequent downtown New York jazz clubs to hear and sometimes talk with performers including Dizzy Gillespie, Sonny Rollins, and Thelonius Monk. Lew admires the "improvisational genius" that he says contributes to good jazz and good basketball alike. Both activities depend upon an openness to possibility. They also require careful and coordinated teamwork, and, when successful, are graceful, fluid, and yet full of excitement.

Lew's passion for baseball predated his love of basketball. He played in little league and was a pitcher on his junior high school team. Although they lived near Yankee Stadium, Lew and his parents were avid fans of the Brooklyn Dodgers. In the early 1950s, Lew and his mother would listen together to games on the radio, and, on occasion, he and his father would go to Brooklyn, where his father had grown up, to watch games at Ebbets Field. The year Lew was born, Jackie Robinson became the first black to play major league baseball. Far from welcoming him, many fans and players resented Robinson's presence on the Dodgers; the second baseman was subjected to heckling and even to threats. Robinson faced these hateful attacks with remarkable calm. Robinson's consistently cool and dignified demeanor, intense concentration, and quiet competitiveness made him a hero for Lew.

Lew first picked up a basketball during the summer between first and second grade. In the early mornings, he would go to the gym at P.S. 52, the public school where he began first grade. The older kids who showed up afterwards were amused to see the skinny but not yet especially tall boy struggle to heave the ball high enough to reach the backboard.

Three years later, Lew was in the fourth grade and had just begun to attend a boarding school outside of Philadelphia. The year was difficult in many respects. He was living away from his parents for the first time. Setting education as a very high priority, Lew's parents had already impressed upon Lew the importance of books and school. Since many of his schoolmates were not so lucky, Lew's academic abilities proved to be a very mixed blessing. His teachers used him as an example to the others; one even made him read aloud for a seventh grade class. Not surprisingly, his good grades and the attention and praise that teachers gave to Lew made other students feel hostile towards him; he was teased, threatened, and even beat up.

Fitting in was even harder since, by this time, Lew's size made him stand out. At 5′8″, he was the second tallest student in the whole school, which went through eighth grade. But during the year, he gained at least some sense of belonging when some of the older boys recognized that Lew's height had certain advantages. They started to include him in their tough and physical games of basketball, games which Lew said included elements of basketball, lacrosse and prizefighting. He joined the school team, which often practiced and played at a local seminary since the school didn't have a gym of its own. Having not yet really begun to develop essential strength and skills, Lew didn't get much court time that year. Once, when he was closely covered by an opponent and had his back to the basket, he looked over his shoulder and launched his first hook. Even though he didn't make a basket that time, the shot that was to become his signature somehow felt right. Never taught to make the shot, Lew began to practice what had started as a natural response to pressures of a game. The skyhook had been born. When his parents recognized that boarding school was making Lew somewhat cool and aloof, they decided that he should return to St. Jude's for fifth grade. St. Jude's was a Catholic school in Inwood that Lew had previously attended. Lew began working with Farrell Hopkins, the tireless coach of all sports at St. Jude's.

Lew Alcindor was an excellent student and graduated high school with an 85 average.

Coach Hopkins urged Lew to try out for the basketball team, but he also advised Lew not to take his height for granted. He insisted that Lew learn and develop the fundamental skills necessary to play a consistently effective game. Although Lew and his teammates enjoyed attempting outrageous shots and dazzling plays when Hopkins wasn't watching, Lew would also do layups in the gym long after others had gone home. He also began to run track to increase his speed on the court.

In seventh grade, Lew began to wear the number 33 when Coach Hopkins managed to get new uniforms for the team. Having previously worn the number 5, Lew decided on 33 because it was the number of New York Giant Mel Tippet, who was Lew's favorite football player. Little did he know then that he would wear the number for the rest of his basketball career.

Along with new uniforms came Lew's increasing understanding of the ugly reality of racism. His father explained to him that the reason that they went to Harlem for haircuts was that some barbers in Inwood might not cut their hair correctly or might not even want to cut it at all. "This didn't shock me or anything," Lew wrote later in a *Sports Illustrated* essay. "It just gave me something to think about, and I digested it in my mind for several days. That's the way racial knowledge comes to American black children, a little at a time, some of it digestible and some of it as hard to take as rocks in the stomach, until that dull pain becomes constant and you can't get rid of it. It starts with things like the long bus ride for a haircut."

In sixth and seventh grade, Lew became conscious of other acts and expressions of prejudice. At lunch one day, white classmates were horrified by one student's suggestion that they would turn black if they put charcoal on their faces. This left Lew to ask himself why the possibility was so terrible to them. And Lew and a white schoolmate, who had been his best friend in his early years of school, began to grow apart. One afternoon, while he was walking home from school, the friend came up behind Lew and called him "nigger" over and over again. Except for an angry retort, Lew never spoke to the friend again. Lew came to realize that this friend's offensive behavior had been influenced by the racist attitudes of his family and schoolmates. But prejudice helped turn Lew into a loner at school.

Basketball at St. Jude's continued to provide Lew with an important outlet. During eighth grade, he grew to 6'8". In a moment that Lew still vividly remembers, he made his first dunk shot after receiving a pass on the fast break from a teammate. St. Jude's rarely boasted a strong basketball team, but that year they beat perennial powerhouse Good Shepherd to share the district title. Lew scored 33 points in the game. Although the St. Jude's team did not manage to win the league championship, Lew and two teammates played and won a three-man city tournament held in Central Park. The trophy was Lew's first as well as the first for St. Jude's. Lew says that the pride and thrill he experienced over that event have never been equalled in his career.

Lost games may have been as important as victories to Lew's development as a player; at

St. Jude's, winning trophies did not come easy. Lew would lead his high school and college teams in remarkable, record-setting winning streaks. But at St. Jude's Lew learned not just to revel in victory, but also to persevere with pride and confidence even when final scores were not in his favor.

3
PLAYING AT POWER

Lew's height and talent attracted the attention of a number of high schools. Among those recruiting him was Power Memorial High School, a Catholic boys school located on the West Side of Manhattan about 150 blocks downtown from Lew's home. Lew accepted Power's scholarship offer because the school was strong in academics as well as sports and because he liked Jack Donahue, their basketball coach.

Lew entered his freshman year at Power in the fall of 1961. He started that school year playing on the varsity team. The Panthers lost the first game in which he played; Lew could not figure out how to stop an opposing all-City guard from making shot after shot. But Lew used the exposure to older, more experienced

Alcindor set New York City records by scoring 2,067 points and pulling down 2,002 rebounds in his high school career. In 1964, Lew led Power Memorial to its second straight undefeated season, second New York City title, and first national high school championship.

Jack Donohue went on to coach Holy Cross College and the Canadian Olympic team, after he coached the young Alcindor.

players as an opportunity to sharpen his own skills, to fight feelings of intimidation, and to develop a more aggressive game. Now 6'10", he became Power's starting center. As Lew developed, his opponents began to have serious trouble defending against him. One frustrated player even resorted to biting Lew's arm. Although Power lost in the Catholic high school finals that year, defeat soon became a thing of the past.

The Panthers began a remarkable winning streak during Lew's sophomore year. They won every game and, for the first time since 1939, claimed the Catholic City championship title. That year Lew, now 7'0", averaged 19 points and 18 rebounds a game. Power's games began attracting large crowds, and Lew began drawing media attention. But Coach Donahue strictly limited the press's access to Lew.

The next year, Power again won every game and claimed the championship title. During Lew's senior year, Power's extraordinary 71-game winning streak was finally broken; the Panthers lost one game to their archrival, De Matha Catholic High School. But this loss was their only one, and Power went on to attain the New York City Catholic championship title for the third year in a row. Lew finished his high school career with 2,067 points, which was a city record.

In the summer, Coach Donahue ran Friendship Farm, a basketball camp for boys in upstate New York. The large amount of time that Lew spent playing basketball at the camp helped his game, but he found the experience at camp difficult and lonely. "I was supposed to be at the camp to have a good time — at least that's what I'd been told — but how are you supposed to have a good time with a bunch of Irish and Italian Catholic kids who think you stink, and not a single black brother or sister within miles?" Lew asked years later. Occasionally, Lew and a camper were able to get past stereotypes in order to achieve some degree of understanding. But this seemed the exception rather than the rule.

One summer, Lew decided not to go to basketball camp. He began working as a sports journalist in a workshop run by the Harlem Youth Action Project. He researched articles at the Schomburg Center for Research in Black Culture and covered a press conference of Martin Luther King, Jr., whose philosophy of nonviolence Lew has since come to believe is "probably the only way." Once, on his way to observe a protest rally, he emerged from the subway into the midst of the first night of a bloody riot that had begun after a white off-duty policeman had shot and killed a black high school student. Covering the riot for the paper in the following days, he began to understand it as an expression of the powerlessness of black Americans in a culture where the killing that had sparked it was sadly more typical than unique.

That same summer, Coach Donahue strongly urged Lew to come back to the camp, admitting how important his star student was in attracting other campers. Finally, Lew agreed to return to Friendship Farm. But feeling anything but friendly and despite his celebrity status, Lew continued to regard himself as an outsider and alone.

During Lew's junior year, Power was playing a Bronx team in a game that they should have easily won. Although they were leading by six points at halftime, Power, and especially Lew, had performed poorly in the first half. Coach Donahue started rebuking his players for their performances. Eventually he turned to Lew and said, "And you! You go out there and don't hustle. You don't move. You don't do any of the things you're supposed to do. You're acting just like a nigger!"

Lew, feeling shocked, went on to finish the game, though he remembers nothing about it. He remained at Power. But he decided that after high school he would not follow Donahue, who had a number of colleges interested in hiring him. Lew credits Donahue with teaching him a great deal. Coach Donahue's consistently high expectations had a profound effect upon Lew. But after the Coach's outburst, nothing between Donahue and Lew was ever quite the same.

More happy than those of summer camp are Lew's memories of time spent watching and playing basketball on New York City playgrounds. From an early age, Lew and his friends would travel with their basketballs to foreign asphalt courts, where they would play and watch older and more experienced players compete. When he got to high school age, Lew became a fan of the Rucker Tournament, in which pro players met city playground stars in intensely competitive and spirited games. There he saw greats including Wilt Chamberlain and Connie Hawkins. He also played in the Tournament, facing off for the first time against the future Hall of Famer Julius Erving.

Participating in playground matches, Lew was introduced into what he describes as "subculture of competition and playground excellence," a subculture whose members pushed to excel and drew crowds amazed by the energy and exhilaration of the games.

Throughout high school, Lew also attended lots of professional games at Madison Square Garden, for Donahue often got tickets that he would share with his players. Although Lew rooted for his hometown team, the New York Knicks were not a very successful team in those days. At Coach Donahue's urging, when the Knicks met Boston, Lew always devoted special attention to watching Celtic center Bill Russell. In addition to Russell's techniques for passing and for blocking shots, Russell's willingness to sacrifice individual glory to contribute to the strength and success of his team made a lasting impression upon Lew.

Lew's expertise on the court, coupled with a solid academic record, earned Lew admission and scholarships to any number of colleges. He considered St. John's in New York, where Joe Lapchick was coach. Lew respected the way that Lapchick stressed basketball as an outlet for the development of character. But Lapchick decided to retire, and Lew grew most interested in UCLA and the University of Michigan. He first visited UCLA and then Michigan during the spring of his senior year of high school. Impressed by the people he met at UCLA, the basketball team, UCLA Coach John Wooden, and the California campus, Lew decided to leave New York for the West.

4

THE WINNING CONTINUES

Lew's freshman basketball team at UCLA opened Pauley Pavilion in the fall of 1965 with a game against the university's varsity team. History was being made in more ways than one. UCLA's new sports facility had been planned for 17 years. The night of the game, the 12,500-seat arena received its very first crowd of fans. Since the varsity team had won the national championship the previous spring and was ranked first in pre-season college polls, everybody at the game expected the older team to win. But no one had seen these fresh men play together. With Kenny Heitz, Kent Taylor, Lynn Shackleford, Lucius Allen, and Lew, the freshmen won the game by 15 points. A new era in college basketball had begun.

If Lew's college basketball career got off to a

Prior to Alcindor's arrival, coach John Wooden had directed UCLA to back-to-back national championships in 1964-65. Wooden was already in the Basketball Hall of Fame due to his achievements as a player at Purdue University and in the pros.

flying start, other aspects of his life were more strained. He had hoped that California would be a place of greater racial tolerance, acceptance, and equality. Lew reflected shortly after he graduated from UCLA, "I had to face the fact that there was prejudice in New York, and there was a semipermanent riot situation in the Harlem I once loved. Maybe it was better to get away from all that for a while and go out to California, where people were color-blind and a man could live his life without reference to color or race."

Within days of his arrival at college, his high expectations were disappointed. He learned that for the most part the student population at UCLA was anything but colorblind. Interaction between white and black students seemed to take place only on superficial levels.

Lew found that his most significant friendships were with other black male students. His freshman year roommate was Lucius Allen, who would later be a teammate on both the Bucks and the Lakers. He spent a lot of time with UCLA varsity player Edgar Lacey, whom he viewed as a "very thoughtful, sensitive brother." Another friend was J. J. Johnson, who excelled academically at UCLA and went on to Harvard Law School.

Reading books and sharing ideas in "bull sessions" with his friends became an important pastime for Lew. During his freshman year, he first read *The Autobiography of Malcolm X* and became deeply interested in African-American history and the Islamic religion that Malcolm followed.

Though Lew had been a practicing Catholic all of his life, he didn't go to mass after reaching

Lew Alcindor made his college debut in 1965 as the UCLA freshmen—the greatest college freshman team ever—played the UCLA varsity.

UCLA. He sensed that his views and feelings about religion were shifting. He read all that he could about Islam, including the Koran, the sayings of Mohammed and the histories of Islam. The brand of Islam that Malcolm X ultimately recognized held that all men, black and white, are brothers. Lew could understand but could not finally embrace the rage that some black Americans feel towards whites. Many years later, he described the development of his position: "Emotionally, spiritually, I could not afford to be a racist. As I got older, I got past believing that black was either the best or the worst. It just was." Lew's increasingly strong

coil, launch yourself into the air, extend your arm, lengthen your body, and then release the ball. You can't defend against it; nobody can get a hand on it...." Lew makes it sound easy, and, when Lew received the ball on a pass and shot over his shoulder, he made it look even easier. But shooting with your back to the basket from considerable distances requires incredible concentration, touch, and coordination. Lew's air of ease, the gentle twist and extension of his body, and the arc of the ball as it travelled to the basket, all contributed to make the shot one of the most graceful basketball plays ever made. But though he executed the hook with the poise of a dancer, he also used it to defy the fiercest of defenders; since the ball was released while Lew was turned away from the man guarding him, the ball was too high to be blocked by the time it got within the horizontal range of the defender.

During the summer of his sophomore year, Lew returned to New York City and a job with the New York City Housing Authority. Working with Knicks players Emmette Bryant and Freddie Crawford, Lew visited housing projects, talked with kids about basketball, and showed them some of his own shots and moves. He also spoke with them about black pride. Lew got paid $5,000 for his work. More importantly, he felt that he was getting through to the young people with whom he talked and played.

When Lew returned to UCLA as a junior, the dunk shot had been banned in college games. His ability to drop the ball in the basket without jumping had provided Lew with a big advantage, and now he would have to play without this important piece of ammunition.

Lew felt the ban was instituted in order to check his dominance in the game. But with Coach Wooden's guidance and encouragement, Lew more than compensated for his loss. His form became more graceful and his on-court strategy improved.

During Lew's junior year, UCLA lost only one game — but it was their first in two years! Eight days before a game against the University of Houston, the cornea of Lew's left eye was badly scratched during a game. In order to help his eye heal, he spent a few days in a dark room at the UCLA eye clinic with a patch over his eyes.

Although he played the whole time against Houston, Lew's game was totally off; he felt drained and had trouble with his depth perception, and, for the first time in his college career, he made less than fifty percent of his shots. With their center Elvin Hayes playing a great game, Houston claimed a 71-69 victory.

For the rest of the season, the media ranked Houston first and UCLA second. This really inflamed Lew and his teammates, but Coach Wooden had confidence that UCLA would meet Houston again. To keep himself charged up, Lew kept a *Sports Illustrated* cover over his locker that showed Elvin Hayes reaching over Lew's head to shoot a basket.

Sure enough, UCLA met Houston again in March at the NCAA semifinals, which were held

In 1968, Elvin Hayes was named college player of the year as he averaged 36.8 points and 18.9 rebounds per game. Here he shoots over Alcindor in the University of Houston's huge upset that allowed the Wildcats to win their 49th straight home victory.

in Los Angeles. Hayes tried to distract Lew by talking trash, but Lew was too busy to listen. The Bruins clobbered Houston by 32 points. In an expression of black pride, Lew left the locker room wearing a bright African robe. The Bruins went on to defeat the University of North Carolina in the finals and to earn their second NCAA title.

Perhaps the biggest challenge of Lew's junior year was managing the controversy that surrounded his participation in the 1968 Olympics boycott. He and other black athletes in the United States agreed that a boycott would be a powerful statement of their outrage against the climate of racism in the United States. As Lew reports, "We didn't want any more of that stuff where Cassius Clay walks into a restaurant with his Olympic gold medal around his neck and can't get a glass of orange juice. If white America behaved that way, then white America could win the Olympics on its own." Many people in the media harshly criticized him for this position.

Instead of going to Mexico City for the Olympic Games during the summer of 1968, Lew returned to New York City and Operation Sports Rescue. Lew talked with inner-city children about the importance of staying in school, finishing their education, and staying off drugs. Lew believed that the sort of direct connection he could make with young people was a far more important contribution to the country than an Olympic medal ever could be.

When Alcindor decided not to play for the U.S. Olympic team in 1968, he accepted the offer from the New York City Housing Authority to put on basketball clinics for children of low-income families. In Long Island City, Alcindor shows how to hold the ball for a dunk shot as Freddie Crawford (right rear) looks on.

That summer, Lew made another important life decision. After receiving intensive religious instruction in a Harlem mosque, Lew made a commitment to Islam. As part of his conversion, he changed his name from Lew Alcindor to Kareem Abdul-Jabbar. Kareem means "noble and generous" and Jabbar means "powerful." These are attributes of the supreme being, Allah. Abdul, which means "servant," indicates that he does not put himself on the same level as the supreme being.

At first, Kareem was very private about his conversion and only those close to him knew about his new name. But he eventually shared the news of his conversion with his UCLA teammates when the team was on a bus travelling from Columbus, Ohio, to South Bend, Indiana, for a game against Notre Dame University. Coach Wooden and the team listened and at first were quiet. When conversation resumed, Kareem realized that they had accepted his decision.

During Kareem's senior year, UCLA lost only one game. In the last game of the regular season, USC beat the Bruins by a score of 46-44. It was Kareem's only loss in Pauley Pavilion. Still, the team didn't stay down for long. Instead, they went on to win the national championship, becoming the first team in history to win three consecutive NCAA titles. Kareem was chosen most valuable player in each of the championship tournaments. In Kareem's three years on the varsity team, the Bruins won 88 games and lost only two.

In 1969, Kareem received a degree in history. He now stood 7'2", and was ready for the pros.

5

KAREEM ENTERS THE PROS

Kareem had hoped to play with the New York Knicks. But the Milwaukee Bucks won the right to draft Kareem, and they made Kareem an attractive five-year offer. He also received an offer from the American Basketball Association's New York Nets, but it was not as good a deal as the Bucks offered.

The Milwaukee Bucks were a new team; they were just entering their second NBA season, and they had ended their first in second to last place. Expectations for the team were not too high, but even before the 1969-70 regular season began, Kareem's presence and performance helped to stir enthusiasm and confidence among everyone. His size, speed, and skill excited the crowds and caused big problems for opponents. In Kareem's first season, he helped his team win 19 more games than in the previous year; the Bucks enjoyed a season of 56 wins and only 26 losses. Kareem scored

As a young Buck, Kareem Abdul-Jabbar had to take on the legend of Wilt Chamberlain.

more points than anyone in the NBA that season, and, averaging 28.8 points a game, ended up with a scoring average higher than everyone but Laker Jerry West. On defense, Kareem stayed near the basket to block shot after shot of opponents who attempted to work inside the lane. Kareem was named NBA rookie of the year.

The Bucks reached the playoffs and beat the Philadelphia 76ers in the Eastern Division semifinals; they scored a record 156 points in the third game of the series. They met New York in the Division finals, and Kareem faced off against Knick center Willis Reed. Although the Knicks beat the Bucks in a five-game series, Kareem later reflected on how much progress his team made during the 1969-70 season. "That wasn't a punishing defeat for us because we had gone farther than anyone expected. We went from being the doormat of the league to being a very good team."

Off court life also involved some adjustments for Kareem. He did not relish Wisconsin's dark and bitter winters. But even more difficult to handle than the weather was the way of life that seemed prevalent in the Milwaukee. Kareem described himself as a "strange object" at whom people would "gawk and point." Afflicted by what he later called "serious culture shock" upon moving to what seemed to him to be a quiet, slow-paced midwestern town, Kareem badly missed the music, the excitement, and diversity of people and lifestyles that New York and Los Angeles had to offer.

The next season, Kareem was overjoyed when the Bucks acquired Oscar Robertson through a trade with the Cincinnati Royals. The 10-year NBA veteran guard was an amazing all-around player. He was no longer a super potent scoring threat, but his passing skills would be particularly important to Kareem's game. When the Bucks had the ball, Kareem's job as center was to run down court and fight for a position near the basket. The guard's job was to get him the ball in good position to score or pass to an open man. Robertson could get the ball to him at just the right time and place; Jabbar once said, "No way not to score when Oscar was around."

Despite his stellar record in the NBA, the 32-year old Robertson had yet to play on a championship team, and he arrived eager to help the Bucks win a title. Along with Robertson, Lucius Allen also joined the Bucks that season. Allen and Kareem were friends, having been teammates at UCLA; they already knew how to play well together. The Bucks' roster also included Jon McGlocklin, Bobby Dandridge, and Greg Smith. The team specialized in a fast-running game.

By the time of the season opener against the Atlanta Hawks, the coordinated playing of Kareem and Robertson had already drawn a lot of attention. Thanks to Robertson's assists, Kareem scored 32 points in that game, and the Bucks won 107-98. The Bucks were off and running for the season, and they went on to win game after game. They enjoyed a 20-game winning streak, breaking the 18 game record that the Knicks had established during the previous season. The Bucks finished the season with a 66-16 record. They led the Western Conference, in which they were placed when the NBA's

In basketball, a "triple-double" is when a player racks up double figures in three separate categories in one game. In 1961-62, Oscar Robertson posted a triple-double average for the season by scoring 30.8 points, pulling down 12.5 rebounds and dishing out 11.4 assists. Robertson was past his prime when he came to the Bucks, but he still drew double teams (here, Fred Carter, left, and Earl Monroe).

structure was rearranged before the season began, and they won 14 more games than the Knicks, who led the Eastern Conference.

In the first round of the playoffs, the Bucks took four of the five games that they played with the San Francisco Warriors. They met the Lakers for the Western Division title, where they took four out of five games with a margin of at least 18 points a game. It looked for a while as if they would compete with the Knicks for the NBA title, but New York was edged out by the Baltimore Bullets in the seventh game of the Eastern Conference finals. And so the Bucks faced Baltimore in the NBA championship tournament.

Wes Unseld was the Bullets' starting center. Despite being only 6′9″, he led the league in rebounds. The faster and much taller Abdul-Jabbar didn't leave many rebounds to collect, though. The Bucks swept the series, winning each game by at least eight points. Only once before had a team managed to win all of the games in a NBA championship series.

Kareem led the league in scoring, with a 31.7 point average in the regular 1970-71 season. He was named most valuable player in the playoffs and in the league.

Later that year, Kareem made other significant steps. In May, he married Janice Brown, a Washington, D.C. school teacher; the two had met in California when Kareem was at UCLA. And that summer, he demonstrated the extent of his commitment to Islam by legally adopting the name Kareem Abdul-Jabbar.

Although they won 63 regular season games, the Bucks were unable to defend their title in 1972. With Bill Sharman as a new coach, and a rejuvenated Wilt Chamberlain playing center, the Los Angeles Lakers rocketed to achieve a startling success. With 69 victories and only 13 defeats, the Lakers finished the season with the best NBA won lost record ever. The Bucks, handicapped by injuries to Robertson, lost to the Lakers in a six-game Western Conference finals series.

Once again, Kareem was elected the league's most valuable player. He had the league's highest scoring average (34.8) and third highest rebounding average (16.6).

Kareem's first daughter was born shortly after the playoffs ended that year. She was given the name Habiba, which her mother had also taken. Kareem studied Arabic that summer at Harvard University.

More medical problems plagued the Bucks during the 1972-73 season. Robertson had pains in his toe at the beginning of the season and later he pulled a shoulder muscle. Guard Wali Jones also had to be placed on indefinite medical suspension.

Despite these obstacles, the Bucks won 60 regular season games to tie the Lakers for the best Western Conference record. In the first round of the playoffs, the Bucks met the Golden State Warriors, a team they were expected to beat. The Warriors' Nate Thurmond closely guarded Kareem and managed to keep him from making the big points that the Bucks needed. The Bucks were eliminated from the playoffs, losing four games to two.

In the 1973-74 season, Kareem and Allen worked together to help the Bucks achieve the best record in the Western Conference. A few days before the end of the season, Allen suffered a knee injury that sidelined him for the rest of the year. But the rest of the team pulled together and managed through skill and sweat to compensate for the loss. They trounced the Lakers and the Chicago Bulls in the early rounds of the playoffs, taking eight of the nine games they played in the two series. But the real test was still before them. In what was to become one of the most famous finals series ever, the Bucks met the Boston Celtics. Kareem, now acknowledged as the league's best center, faced Boston's Dave Cowens, a fierce competitor in his own right. The Celtics had finished their season with a 56-26 record and had easily beaten the Knicks and the Bullets in the

Although Kareem was five inches taller than Boston's starting center, Dave Cowens got a lot of help from his teammates in the seventh game of the 1973 finals, and the Celtics won 102-87.

playoffs. They hadn't been in the finals since 1969, and they were eager for a championship title.

The incredible series lasted seven games. Boston won the opening game at Milwaukee, but the Bucks won the second game in overtime. Each team claimed a victory in the following two games in Boston. When the Celtics won the fifth game in Milwaukee, it seemed that they would be able to clinch the title in the sixth game on their home court. But, the Celtics had to be satisfied with a tie at the end of regulation—and a tie at the end of overtime. In double overtime, with seven seconds remaining, Boston was leading by 1 point. During a time out, the Bucks decided to direct the ball to

McGlocklin for a jump shot since they figured that Kareem would be tightly covered. But when Jon could not get free, Kareem took a pass at the free throw line, dribbled to the baseline, and propelled a winning hookshot. The Bucks had won the game by a score of 102-101. Despite the Bucks' home-court advantage in the seventh game of the series, however, the Celtics' teamwork secured them a 102-87 victory and the NBA championship title.

Kareem's last season on the Bucks was an anticlimax. Robertson retired from the team, and his presence was sorely missed. Greg Smith, perhaps Kareem's closest friend on the team, was traded to the Houston Rockets the year before. And Lucius Allen was traded 10 games into the season. Things just didn't feel the same. What really made the season a tough one, though, for both Kareem and the Bucks, was an injury he sustained in an exhibition game. Once again, his eye was scratched by an opponent grabbing for the ball in a rebound struggle. Reacting from the physical pain and the frustration of another injury, Kareem punched the backboard's metal support and broke two bones in his right hand. Though his eye was all right in a few days, his hand took six weeks to heal. As a result, he missed the first 16 games of the season.

When he returned to the game, he was wearing the protective goggles that have since become a trademark. Never again would he risk injuring an eye. After six corneal abrasions, he would not play the game without the eye gear with which he is now associated. With Kareem out of commission for so many games, 1975 turned out to be a losing season for the Bucks, the first that Kareem had experienced since St. Jude's. As a star on a team unable to rise to a championship, Kareem finally decided that it was time for him to move on. He asked to be traded. He tried to return to New York to play with the Knicks, but a suitable deal could not be struck. In June, the Bucks closed a deal with the Los Angeles Lakers. Kareem was traded for four players—Junior Bridgeman, Dave Meyers, Brian Winters, and Elmore Smith. These players were all younger than the 28-year-old Kareem. But, as it turned out, Kareem stayed in the pros after all these others were gone.

Though excited about moving back to Los Angeles and playing championship ball with a team of the Lakers' distinction, Kareem had mixed feelings about leaving his many Milwaukee fans. "When I left Milwaukee," Kareem later recalled, "I left with their good will, a championship ring, and some friendships that have lasted. I also left with a new name for my shot." Kareem and his skyhook were again heading west.

6 RETURNING WEST

The Lakers needed help. Since winning the 1972 championship, the team had lost stars Wilt Chamberlain and Jerry West. In the 1974-75 season, the team won only 30 games. In his first season as a Laker, Kareem worked with Coach Bill Sharman and teammates including Gail Goodrich and Cazzie Russell to start turning things around. From the start, Kareem played outstanding ball in Los Angeles. The Laker offense began to revolve around him dominating the inside. Not only could Kareem shoot; he could also pass. So, if a defense was smothering him, Kareem would pass the ball to a teammate who had a clearer shot.

The system worked. In the 1975-76 season, Kareem was second in scoring, with a total of 2,275 points and a 27.7 point per game aver-

Bill Walton followed in Kareem's footsteps at UCLA and led the Bruins to an NCAA-record 87 consecutive victories. In 1977, Walton's Portland Trailblazers swept the Lakers and went on to win the NBA championship by beating Julius Erving's Philadelphia 76ers.

In Magic Johnson's first game as a Laker, he hugged a surprised Kareem after Kareem hit a last-minute winning shot. Such joy sparked the Lakers and the formerly dour Kareem. "Magic baptized him," said coach Paul Westhead. "He transferred him into an enthusiastic player, because in our last game against Seattle [in the 1980 playoffs] it was Kareem running over to Magic when it was over and picking him up."

age. He also played awesome defensive ball, with 100 more blocked shots and 200 more defensive rebounds than any other player. Kareem was chosen most valuable player. The Lakers just missed a playoff spot that year, but they were on their way.

The next year, with Kareem again in control and former guard Jerry West as new head coach, the Lakers enjoyed a winning season. They claimed 53 wins to earn the best record in the league. In the Western Conference finals, the Portland Trailblazers, led by Bill Walton, devastated the Lakers' championship hopes by sweeping the series. This season, Kareem came in second to Walton in rebounds and blocked shots. Nevertheless, having established his overall dominance and carrying much of the responsibility on his team, Kareem was once again elected most valuable player of the league.

Two minutes into the first game of the 1977-78 season, Kareem got into a fight with Milwaukee rookie Kent Benson. Benson elbowed Kareem so hard that Kareem lost his breath. Livid, Kareem responded by punching Benson in the head. Kareem was fined but not suspended—there was no need, for he had broken his hand.

Kareem's injury would keep him out of 20 games. Now 30 years old, he used the time off to assess the state of his life. He began to realize how much enjoyment and satisfaction he sacrificed by keeping such a distance from others. In his autobiography *Giant Steps*, Kareem wrote, "I realized, with my hand broken and reputation damaged, that my temper could ruin my career and that I'd have to control it, but Cheryl Pistono [a friend who later became his second wife] went deeper and told me that I was missing out on not only my career but my whole peace of mind. I had stopped caring to the point that though I could not feel pain, I could also not be pleased, wasn't there to hurt or to love."

Outward change was gradual, and continued long after he had successfully resumed playing. But Kareem became more open to people and experience. He began to establish closer contact with his parents, from whom he had become distant over the years; he began to send his parents greetings during television interviews.

Kareem's relationship with the media, which at times had been tense, also improved. In high school and college, his coaches and athletic departments intervened to limit interviews with Kareem. When he got to the pros, he felt uncomfortable with reporters, and they sometimes reacted negatively to his reserve. He felt that he was sometimes misunderstood. In his most recent autobiography, *Kareem*, he described how this eventually began to change: "I've outlasted my most severe critics. And I've come to a better understanding of how my own wariness, the caution I developed so young, drew the wariness of others toward me. I've made a conscious effort to stop generalizing about the motives of the press, and I've found that if I give them a chance, they give me one too, and that seems to work out better for both of us."

In each of the 1977-78 and the 1978-79 season, the Lakers had winning records and managed to reach the playoffs, but they were stopped before the finals. Then, in 1979, a rookie named Earvin "Magic" Johnson, Jr. joined the team.

Along with incredible strength, versatility, and passing ability, Magic had an incredible energy and enthusiasm for the game and for his team. In the first regular game of the season, Kareem launched a long skyhook to win a game against the San Diego Clippers as the buzzer sounded. Magic went absolutely wild, jumping and hugging Kareem. The veteran had to remind the rookie of the long road ahead; he recalls telling Magic, "We can't be at this emotional pitch for the whole season or we won't make it to Thanksgiving."

But Magic's zest infected his team. The Lakers played hard and won. Achieving 60 regular season victories and breezing through the early rounds of playoffs against the Phoenix Suns and the Seattle Supersonics, the Lakers entered the finals to take on the Philadelphia 76ers, led by Julius Erving. The 76ers, who would be the Lakers' chief rival during the early 1980's, were favored; they had beaten the Lakers in each of the four regular season games in which the teams had met.

The Lakers and the 76ers split the first four games. In the third quarter of Game Five, Kareem badly injured his ankle; team doctors told him that it was the worst sprain they had ever seen. But Kareem made a heroic effort; he went back into the game with his ankle taped and, although in pain, he led his team to a 108-103 victory. Despite his injury, he scored 40 points in the game. Kareem was out for Game Six; he remained in Los Angeles while his teammates travelled to Philadelphia. But Magic filled in at center, and the Lakers won by a score of 123-107.

Receiving the championship trophy, Magic said the team had won it for the "big fellow" back in L.A. Johnson was chosen most valuable player of the series. But Kareem was elected most valuable player of the league, thus becoming the only player ever to have received the honor six times. And the decade of Laker dominance had begun.

Between 1981 and 1986, the Laker team twice more claimed the championship title, reached the finals four times, and participated in the playoffs every year. With Pat Riley as their new head coach, the Lakers again beat Philadelphia in the finals in 1982. In 1985, they at last achieved a championship victory over their long time rival, the Boston Celtics.

Like Kareem and Robertson had done on the Bucks, Kareem and Magic formed an extraordinary partnership. Generally playing point-guard, Magic would typically drive the ball part way down the court. Kareem would stake out a position at the low post, the other Lakers would keep some of the defense busy in the rest of the court, and Magic would pass to Kareem for the basket. In April 1984, when Kareem was about to break Wilt Chamberlain's scoring record in a game against the Utah Jazz, there was no ques-

In 1983, Jabbar's house burned down, leaving him only with the possessions he had packed in his suitcase. Fans across the country, knowing that Kareem loved jazz, sent him thousands of records to help rebuild his once-great collection.

Pat Riley's "Showtime" was basketball at its most exciting. Kareem was called upon to score, rebound, and to throw the outlet passes that got the fast break started.

tion about how he had to do it. Magic entered the game and passed to Kareem, who sank one of his signature skyhooks. With the shot, Kareem achieved a career total of 31,422 regular season points and became the NBA's all-time leading scorer. His record has never been broken.

In 1987, Coach Pat Riley revised the Laker strategy to provide a more balanced offense. The team included Kareem, Magic, James Worthy, Byron Scott, Michael Cooper, A. C. Green, and Mychal Thompson. Opponents had begun to figure out ways to defend against the

Lakers inside game. So, although they still counted on Kareem's presence near the low post and Magic's in the backcourt, the Lakers began to concentrate more on their perimeter game.

The fast, lively, and creative playing mode of Laker play that developed during these years became known as "show time." In his book *Show Time*, Coach Riley described some of the defining features of the style: "excitement, constantly running, scoring explosively, elevating the transition game to an art. Skyhooks, fast breaks, thread-the needle no-look passes, slam dunks, high fives."

Showtime helped secure the Lakers back-to-back championship titles. In 1987, they beat the Celtics again, this time in a six-game series. After winning in 1987, Riley made a bold pledge—he guaranteed that his team would repeat their championship victory the next year. With 62 regular season wins, the Lakers easily reached the playoffs in 1988. The playoffs proved more difficult—each of the last three playoff rounds, including the finals series against the Detroit Pistons, went seven games. The Lakers refused to succumb to the pressure and exhaustion, however, and, upon beating Detroit, they became the first team to win consecutive titles since 1969.

7

GOODBYE

The time had finally come. As hard as it was for basketball enthusiasts truly to grasp, the 1988-89 season would be Kareem's last. He had thought about leaving after the 1984-85 season, but Jerry West had convinced him he could help his team to further championships. But this time, retirement was real.

As the season progressed, he realized that he had returned prepared "to contribute, but not to dominate." "I was in shape," he says, "but I wasn't crisp, and the underlying conditioning wasn't there." A badly bruised knee kept him out for seven games, and some critics called for him to retire earlier than planned. Kareem persisted, pledging to work even harder and, ultimately, helping his team to another winning record and spot in the playoffs.

On his farewell tour, Kareem received standing ovations and presents everywhere he went. In Seattle, the Supersonics gave him a lounge chair and a painting—and Magic Johnson and the rest of the Lakers wore Abdul-Jabbar masks that also adorned all the floorside seats.

Kareem has kept very active following his retirement. He has acted in a number of movies, including the very funny Airplane!

The Lakers swept Portland, Seattle, and Phoenix in the first three rounds of the playoffs. In the finals, they again faced Detroit. This time, with both Scott and Johnson suffering hamstring injuries, the Lakers were swept in four games.

But there were other gratifications that season. Everyone wanted to give Kareem a special good-bye. New York's Madison Square Garden, where Kareem had once played a high school game, was the first stop in a series of ceremonies that were conducted in his honor at Lakers' road games. Fans at the Garden had not always been friendly to the native New Yorker when he came to take on the Knicks. The night of the farewell ceremony, however, they filled the Garden with shouts of "Kareem" and "Lew" and held up signs saying "Thanks for the memories." Coach Hopkins from St. Jude's and some of his old high school teammates were among those introduced. Kareem received a silver apple, a New York City emblem, and Knick center Patrick Ewing presented him with a framed set of the road jerseys he had worn while at Power, UCLA, Milwaukee, and Los Angeles.

There were many other stops on the farewell tour. In Philadelphia, Julius Erving introduced Kareem as the man who, in Erving's opinion, was the greatest player in NBA history. Kareem was made an honorary Harlem Globetrotter. In Boston, former Celtic coach Red Auerbach presented Kareem with an inscribed chunk of the Boston Garden's parquet floor. Fans, players, and management across the nation found different ways of expressing their deep appreciation and their heartfelt good-byes.

The ceremony in Los Angeles to honor Kareem occurred before the last regular season game. Laker announcer Chick Hearn officiated. He introduced Kareem and Kareem's parents and children to a loudly cheering crowd. There were lots of presentations and gifts. A street next to the Forum was renamed "Kareem Court." President George Bush sent a telegram. Kareem's teammates performed a musical tribute to him after seating him in a giant rocking chair. Then, they presented a Rolls-Royce that they had chosen as a going away gift for Cap, short for Captain and the name Kareem was called by the team. Kareem spoke words of thanks until his voice got hoarse. His son Amir sang the national anthem. All the Lakers returned for the game wearing goggles. To top it all off, the Lakers beat Seattle, 121-117.

Kareem had achieved almost every basketball distinction imaginable, both as an individual and for his team. He played 20 seasons in the NBA—more than anyone else. He was on six world championship teams and named the NBA's most valuable player six times. In a career as demanding and competitive as professional basketball, his very endurance stands as a powerful testament to his ability. So too do the many records that he established; among his NBA records are those for most seasons, games, and minutes played, most points scored, and most blocked shots. He helped make basketball the enormously popular sport that it is today. His grace and dignity lent to the game of basketball a quality of art.

As well as memories to cherish, he had a lot to anticipate. More honors would follow his retirement—both the Lakers and the Bucks retired his jersey, and President Bill Clinton honored him at the National Sports Awards. He is certain to be elected to the Basketball Hall of Fame as soon as he becomes eligible.

Nineteen seconds remained in the fourth game in the finals series against Detroit when the 42-year old center left the Forum court for the very last time. His teammates hugged him. Fans shouted "Kareem" until the game was over. They were trying to offer a fitting final farewell to a legend.

STATISTICS

KAREEM ABDUL-JABBAR

SEASON	TEAM	G	MIN	FGA	FGM	PCT	FTA	FTM	PCT	REB	AST	PTS	AVG
69-70	Milw	82	3534	1810	**938**	.518	743	485	.653	1190	337	**2361**	28.8
70-71	Milw	82	3288	**1843**	**1063**	.577	681	470	.690	1311	272	**2596**	**31.7**
71-72	Milw	81	3583	**2019**	**1159**	.574	732	504	.689	**1346**	370	**2822**	**34.8**
72-73	Milw	76	3254	1772	982	.554	460	328	.713	1224	379	2292	30.2
73-74	Milw	81	3548	1759	948	.539	420	295	.702	1178	386	2191	27.0
74-75	Milw	65	2747	1584	812	.513	426	325	.763	912	264	1949	30.0
75-76	LA	82	3379	1728	914	.529	636	447	.703	**1383**	413	2275	27.7
76-77	LA	82	3016	1533	888	.579	536	376	.701	1090	319	2152	26.2
77-78	LA	62	2265	1205	663	.550	350	274	.783	801	269	1600	25.8
78-79	LA	80	3157	1347	777	.577	474	349	.736	1025	431	1903	23.8
79-80	LA	82	3143	1383	835	.604	476	364	.765	886	371	2034	24.8
80-81	LA	80	2976	1457	836	.574	552	423	.766	821	272	2095	26.2
81-82	LA	76	2677	1301	753	.579	442	312	.706	659	225	1818	23.9
82-83	LA	79	2554	1228	722	.588	371	278	.749	592	200	1722	21.8
83-84	LA	80	2622	1238	716	.578	394	285	.723	587	211	1717	21.5
84-85	LA	79	2630	1207	723	.599	395	289	.732	622	249	1735	22.0
85-86	LA	79	2629	1338	755	.564	439	336	.765	478	280	1846	23.4
86-87	LA	78	2441	993	560	.564	343	245	.714	523	203	1366	17.5
87-88	LA	80	2308	903	480	.532	269	205	.762	478	135	1165	14.6
88-89	LA	74	1695	659	313	.475	165	122	.739	334	74	748	10.1
Totals		**1,560**	**57,446**	**28,307**	**15,837**	.559	9,304	6,712	.721	17,440	5,660	**38,387**	24.6
Playoff Totals		237	8,851	**4,422**	**2,356**	.533	1,419	1,050	.740	2481	767	**5,762**	24.3

G	games
MIN	minutes
FGA	field goals attempted
FGM	field goals made
PCT	percent
FTA	free throws attempted
FTM	free throws made
REB	rebounds
AST	assists
PTS	points
AVG	average

bold indicates league-leading figures

In addition to the records reflected above, Kareem has also set these records:

Most NBA seasons played: 20
Most blocked shots, career: 3,189*
Most personal fouls, career: 4,657
Most times named to All-Star team: 19
Most points scored in All-Star games, career: 251
Most field goals attempted in All-Star games, career: 213
Most field goals made in All-Star games, career: 105
Most blocked shots in All-Star games, career: 31
Most personal fouls in All-Star games, career: 57
Most seasons in NBA playoffs, career: 18

*blocked shots were not officially tabulated before 1973-74 season.

KAREEM ABDUL-JABBAR
A CHRONOLOGY

April 16, 1947   Lew Alcindor born in New York City

1961   Enters Power Memorial High School

1965   Enters UCLA

1967   Leads UCLA to first of three consecutive NCAA titles; is named most outstanding player for the first of three times

1969   Graduates from UCLA; signs with Milwaukee Bucks

1970   Named NBA Rookie of the Year

1971   Leads Bucks over Los Angeles Lakers to win NBA championship; is named most valuable player of championship and of NBA; legally adopts the name Kareem Abdul-Jabbar

1972   Named Most Valuable Player

1974   Named Most Valuable Player

1975   Traded to Los Angeles Lakers

1976   Named Most Valuable Player

1980   Leads Lakers over Philadelphia 76ers to win NBA championship; named Most Valuable Player

1982   Leads Lakers over Philadelphia to win NBA championship

1984   Becomes NBA's leading all-time scorer

1985   Leads Lakers over Boston Celtics to win NBA championship title; named Most Valuable Player; becomes leading all-time scorer in playoffs

1987   Leads Lakers over Boston to win NBA championship

1988   Leads Lakers over Detroit Pistons to win NBA championship

1989   Retires

SUGGESTIONS FOR FURTHER READING

Abdul-Jabbar, Kareem and Knobler, Peter. *Giant Steps.* New York: Bantam Books, 1983.

Abdul-Jabbar, Kareem with McCarthy, Mignon. *Kareem.* New York: Warner Books, 1990.

Haskins, James. *From Lew Alcindor to Kareem Abdul-Jabbar.* Rev. ed. New York: Lothrop, Lee & Shepherd Co., 1978.

Hollander, Zander, and Sachare, Alex, eds. *The Official NBA Basketball Encyclopedia.* New York: Villard Books, 1989.

Riley, Pat. *Show Time.* New York: Warner Books, 1988.

ABOUT THE AUTHOR

A lawyer and graduate student in English literature, Helen Borrello is currently teaching writing at New York University.

INDEX